TROUT

In Pursuit of the World's Most Beautiful Fish

WATER

TROUT

In Pursuit of the World's Most Beautiful Fish

WATER

Jim Rowinski

INTRODUCTION BY

Nick Lyons

Skyhorse Publishing

Skyhorse Publishing books may be purchased in bulk at special discounts for sales promotion, corporate gifts, fund-
raising, or educational purposes. Special editions can also be created to specifications. For details, contact the Special Sales
Department, Skyhorse Publishing, 555 Eighth Avenue, Suite 903, New York, NY 10018 or
info@skyhorsepublishing.com.

www.skyhorsepublishing.com

10 9 8 7 6 5 4 3 2 1

Library of Congress Cataloging-in-Publication Data is available on file.
ISBN: 978-1-61608-138-6

Printed in China

To my grandson Quinn. It is our hope that we can instill in him a love and understanding of trout waters and wild places, for he and his generation hold the key to the future.

Contents

Preface

Lying on the ground as a boy of five or six years, I peered into a side stream of crystal-clear water that split off the main channel of the river where my dad and grandfather were fishing. In it were tiny insects and a few miniature trout. I watched as fry darted and flashed, seemingly jousting with imaginary targets floating within the water. Others stayed stationary in the fast-moving waters, their heads trained directly into the flow, bodies and tails moving in opposing synchronicity with the water's movement. I was mesmerized by that intricate look at the world within their watery world. It wasn't until many years later that I realized that within that tiny rivulet existed the basic ecological principles found in all living trout water.

« *Cool spring-fed pool*

I was certainly not aware of it at the time, but it was to become one of those indelible moments in my life. That small stream, whose name I can no longer recall, helped to create the wonder, passion, and love of trout water that has become a cornerstone in the person I am and helped to make living rivers a part of my life's work.

This book represents a lifetime of living with trout waters. I have tried to convey in photographs and words those sights, smells, sounds, and feelings—stories remembered and forgotten, time away from and shared with special people, daydreams dreamed and aspirations lived, time spent and moments wasted that make up the essential elements of our lives. This is what trout water means to me. This is what trout water has brought to my life.

At its best, trout water is crystal clear and most often wild. Trout need clean, cold water to survive. Like them, I am at my best in clear, wild places. Trout waters play a very important role in my own psychological health and well-being. Without these places, I would be a totally different person, and a much poorer one.

Wild trout streams and rivers are part of the glue that keep me whole and in balance. The more often I can be immersed in and around trout water, the healthier I am. Just knowing they exist is often enough to keep me sane in our fast and high-tech world. It is a feeling I know to be universal, at least for those of us fortunate enough to have felt the crisp snap of a cold morning's cast, or the soft musical patter of a spring creek against our waders on a summer's afternoon. I have shared these moments many times over the years with like-minded souls that I have met on streams and over dinner at the end of a day on the river.

The wildness of trout rivers is as tangible a part of my foundation as the Precambrian rocks beneath my feet. Wild trout waters help to keep me in touch with the heartbeat of the planet. Whether or not we know it, understand it, or even care, our lives are intrinsically intertwined with the life and health of trout waters. They are good barometers of the health of our planet.

Here in North America, we are fortunate to still have a reasonable richness of wild, natural trout water. We have been fortunate to have individuals and organizations over the past hundred years or so who had the vision, the wisdom, and the courage to fight to protect these precious waters. This book is dedicated to all those who have put themselves in the forefront of these battles to save our wild and natural trout waters for future generations. This is the greatest gift you could have given to me—and to the millions of others around our tiny planet earth.

—Jim Rowinski
Charlottesville, VA 2010

Introduction

All trout fishers are different, but we all overlap. The degree to which we share common feelings and dreams, the degree to which we have enjoyed similar experiences, shouldn't surprise me after more than sixty-five years at it—and it really doesn't; but it does always give me a quiet shock of recognition and pleasure. We share, as Jim Rowinski wisely notes, similar "wonder, passion, and love of trout water"—and in many instances, this is the "cornerstone" of who we are, too. Trout water, the kind of water in which trout flourish, is varied, mysterious, and invariably magical, and the photographs in this book, accompanied by Jim Rowinski's sensitive and thoughtful text, enable us to see that world in many of its richest and most memorable configurations.

Though this is a textured portrait in photographs of trout rivers, the text is especially important to this book. The photographs by themselves could become merely decorative and the text without the images potentially arbitrary and dry. The text is excellent—much more personal than similar essays I've read, specific to the rivers the author has loved, knowledgeable about the origins and ecology and discrete forms trout rivers take—and it is intimately linked to the fine photographs. The combination of text and image, though, is more than the sum of its parts; the combination is a new, rich entity.

The history of how rivers are formed, the long gestation period they have undergone to become what they are today, gives us a deeper sense of the continuum of which we, in the twenty-first century, are a part. Rowinski poignantly makes us aware of the genesis of wild rivers, the complex forces, beginning perhaps with rainwater on a mountaintop and then progressing in a rhythmic downward movement until it forms a world that might take many shapes where wild trout can flourish; and he shows how that water then progresses to the ocean, into which the great steelhead venture and then return, bright from their travels.

Tumbling mountain brooks, large freestone rivers, placid and fecund spring creeks, and a dozen other incarnations of living water—these many-faceted rivers don't exist by themselves but in relation to the mountains, canyons, wooded slopes, meadows through which they make their way, and to the seas or lakes into which they inevitably flow. They exist in relation to the human worlds that surround and use them, some kinder than others, and they almost cry out for the fly fishers who come to ply them, to appreciate and understand them (often more intimately than the scientists), to protect them because they have touched their heart. A first trout, the friendships fashioned and grown along the banks of rivers, the fly fishing that grew inevitably from an understanding of ecology and entomology of trout rivers—all of this is here, along with unforgettable portraits, in word and image, of the Wisconsin rivers that Rowinski fished as a boy; Western rivers like the Firehole, Rock Creek, the rivers of the Wind River Range, the Madison, the Gallatin, and the Green; eastern rivers like the Battenkill in Vermont and the famed Beaverkill in the Catskills; the remarkable and challenging spring creeks of Montana's Paradise Valley—Armstrong, DePuy, and Nelson; and the magnificent North Umpqua, home of the great steelhead, so difficult to take, so rewarding to bring to net.

Brook, brown, rainbow, cutthroat, steelhead—all the great American trout are here in their brightest colors. Rowinski shows us the life of the trout, from egg to fry to smolt to magnificent adult, and he shows us the accoutrements of fly fishing—the flies, rods, reels, and clothing.

If the test of great photographs is the degree to which they embed themselves in our memories, I offer these, plucked at random from my brain, far from the images themselves:

a solitary fly fisher checks his fly box on a glassy western river

a huge male brown trout

rivulets from which the great rivers flow

a bright steelhead, the color of polished silver

a small creek alive with insects

a tumbling northern river

a burly bison near a western river

a young deer

two elk in midstream

a brilliant cutthroat

a remote western river and a distinctive spring creek

a fat brook trout

a rainbow in a net

rocks and reflections in a small clear creek

a trout holding in water so clear it seems suspended in air over sunken leaves

Trout Water pulls us deeply into the world of rivers, encourages us to know our obligations to conserve such precious resources, and delights us in sharing a world that all lovers of rivers cherish. It is a personal book. It is a memorable book. It is a book that will strengthen our links to a world we love.

—Nick Lyons
Woodstock, NY 2010

Zealand River, New Hampshire

PART ONE

The Genesis of Trout Water

It is the height of summer in the high country of the Wind River Range. Cumulus clouds build to 30,000 feet above the earth. The jet stream and westerly winds push the cloud masses over Square Top Mountain in Wyoming's Wind River Range, reaching nearly 12,000 feet into the sky.

As the cumulus push across the flattopped peak, the landform acts as a charged lighting rod, changing the electrical forces and causing the moisture-laden clouds to burst with fiery shards of lightning. Thunder boomers echo across the peaks and through the steep valleys of the Range. Rain begins, first as a few drops, then building into a downpour.

Square Top Mountain and Upper Green River, Wyoming

High-mountain cascades

Fire and ice, the sculptors of the landscape

The wind-driven rainwater hits the granite of the mountainside at more than 40 miles per hour as it descends from the cloud mass. Each tiny droplet serves as an almost imperceptible miniature sledgehammer in its effect on the rock. Together, the millions of droplets begin to take their toll, slowly and methodically eroding the granitic rock surfaces.

Green River and Wind River Range, Wyoming

It is not just rain that erodes the rock at these higher elevations. All forms of water follow a continuous pattern of freezing and thawing, adding to the relentless barrage on the solid rock. Eventually, snow and ice accumulate and build into glaciers.

Here in the Wind River Range, some of the largest remaining glaciers in the continental United States slowly grind their way down the steep slopes of granitic rock. Every year, inch by inch, they scrape and sculpt the mountainsides. Glaciers grind the mineral-laden rocks into a rubble of various-size boulders, pebbles, and fine powder.

The Wind River Range is made up of rocks that formed deep under the earth's surface more than 2.8 billion years ago. These hard, dense, granitic rocks are truly the core basement rocks for the North American continent.

For millions of years, the granite backbone that would someday be known as the Rocky Mountains was covered by a large inland sea. Over time, 10,000–20,000 feet of sediment were laid down over the rocks, burying the sleeping giants in layers of organic muck. Eventually this organic layer cake would turn into sedimentary rocks.

Backcountry fly-fishing, Upper Green River, Wind River Range, Wyoming

Beaver pond and jagged peaks of the Grand Tetons, Wyoming

Landing trout in Green River Lake, Wyoming

Around seventy million years ago, as the ocean waters receded, the granite began to awaken once more, pushing upward along fault lines caused by the movement of plates on the earth's crust. Water and river erosion eroded away the softer sedimentary rocks, exposing the granitic batholithic rocks.

Once again, it was the action of water that brought the mountains to life.

About 500,000 years ago, an ice age began to carve the rocks of the range into their current structural shapes. Large Pleistocene glaciers left smaller remnant glaciers that are still present along the flanks of the Wind River Peaks. The erosive effect of these massive "ice rivers" carved the peaks and horns, cirques, arêtes, and U-shaped valleys of the Wind River Range—one of the most rugged, wild, isolated areas left in the continental United States.

Today, as they have for millions of years, the rains wash off the high-elevation rock faces and join with trillions of other droplets to form little rivulets of water. These more concentrated strings of water begin to have a more focused power of erosion. They build into larger torrents that form small, steeply cascading streams that bustle and burst down the mountainsides.

Releasing wild western rainbow trout

Glacier-fed McDonald Creek, Glacier National Park, Montana

Maroon Lake,
Maroon Bells,
Aspen, Colorado

Evening light—Fly-fishing western river

River music—Virginia

Eventually barriers begin to corral the water. Small pools, ponds, and lakes develop. For the most part these are only temporary stopovers until an escape route is found and the waters rush in wild excitement to escape.

Down again through steep cascades and over waterfalls the water leaps into the air, freeborn, frothy white, screaming loudly, then crashing and breaking into a million pieces of spray and splash before settling into another series of calming pools as the velocity of the water begins to slow.

Aqua-green glacial silt-colored water tumbles through the high country of the western river, slowing only as it reaches the plain. Suspended particles begin to drop out of the watery solution. First, the heavier materials like tiny pebbles, then the sediment, and finally the lighter detritus fall to the streambed as the water slows and moves into side eddies, laying the groundwork for a living stream.

As the river slows and drops the suspended particles of this glacial soup, it leaves behind the first minerals that will become the building blocks for new life-forms. These basic minerals will become core ingredients in the creation of new life in every form imaginable; grasses, flowers, trees, insects, fish, birds, and mammals.

Cold and wild western river

As it has from the beginning of time, water is the foundational sculptor of the ever-changing panorama of the American landscape. It flows over and through the country, creating, destroying, and re-creating again the framework of our natural land heritage.

Simple, pure, cold, crystalline water flows over rocks and streambeds, through mountain meadows and primeval forest, past the history of mountain men and a young nation and into the sophistication of our modern day. Imprisoned momentarily by dams or flowing freely and wildly through canyons, these waters are an ever-present heartbeat, carrying with them the past, the present, and the future of life on this planet.

It is here that the wild trout finds its home.

MY FIRST TIME

It seems everyone has a favorite river they call their home river. What is it that makes a river your home river? Is it a place where you first had success or learned to fish? Was it the place that was closest to where you lived and was easily

Landing rainbow trout, Frying Pan River, Colorado

Beautiful rainbow trout about to be released, Blue River, Colorado

*Misty spring
morning stream*

accessible? Did it have something special about it that made you go back time and time again? Were there special fish, memories, or smells that became part of your life? Maybe it became home because of a dad, an uncle, or a good friend who shared time with you there.

*The side pool was
full of tiny trout
darting after
insects . . .*

*The Little Roche a Cri
Creek; Brook trout resting
along stream grasses*

15

Whatever the meaning, home rivers are important for many reasons. My true home rivers are in Wisconsin, where I grew up. The meandering Little Roche a Cri was my first trout stream. I caught my first brook trout there more than forty years ago.

I can still see that moment as if it just happened this morning. I remember crawling up to the little shallow pool, slowly hanging the 8-foot fiberglass fly rod out over the stream so I could release line downstream. Sixteen to 18 feet away, the gray Hare's Ear nymph slowly slid into the top of the pocket pool. *Wham*! My first trout hooked on a fly.

It fought hard, ran all over the tiny stream, but somehow I managed to land it. I cradled it in my hands, 9 or 10 inches, dark, similar to the silty stream bottom; red, yellow, and orange

Vermont waterfall; Ammonoosuc headwaters, New Hampshire

*Dragonfly drying
its wings*

*The greens and reds
of early fall reflections*

circles spread across the mottled dark green sides. I slid it into my wicker creel, then found a patch of long green grass and filled the bottom of my creel with it to keep the trout moist. The sweet smell of the first trout, the grasses, the dampness of the stream edge, the coolness of the morning air all still linger in my memory. How funny, how strange are the ways our minds work.

I have forgotten so many thousands of things over the years that I needed to remember, but those few minutes with that first trout are etched into my brain and memory like they were chiseled into stone.

For a few years, we spent opening weekend on the Little Roche a Cri. It was always good. The fishing, the friends, camping, and eating fresh-caught brook trout for breakfast laid the foundation that somehow turned me into a fly fisherman and a lover of trout and trout waters.

HOME RIVER

It wasn't until I fished my real and lasting home river, the Bois Brule, that I knew my love affair with trout fishing was complete. The Brule starts out in the tamarack and alder bogs near

Solon Springs, Wisconsin, and meanders for nearly 60 miles almost directly north to join Lake Superior. The upper portion of the river is slow-moving, dark-bottomed water draining the tamarack, alder, and spruce forests, the water cola-colored from tangled root systems and dark humus soil.

I have so many memories of days fishing the Brule. I especially remember a campfire date before Kate and I were married. I made her fresh trout, ham, home fries, and toast over an open fire while she sat wrapped in a wool blanket, half wet from getting in and out of the canoe on an early-spring morning paddle. I think it was that morning that I knew she would be my wife.

Blue Ridge Mountain stream—brook trout pool

Brook trout pool, Blue Ridge Mountain stream, Virginia

Roaring Brook,
Vermont

Fall magic on Pemigewasset River, New Hampshire

The Bois Brule is known as the River of Presidents. Five American presidents made the Brule their summer retreat. It is these waters that are my favorite—the middle sections of the river—the waters fished by the presidents. These are areas of cascading pocket water interspersed with small, shallow ponds and miniature lakes within the river itself. They are somewhat unique to the Brule, perhaps reminiscent of the Au Sable in upper Michigan.

Ammonoosuc River,
New Hampshire

It was the first water that tested my skills as a fly fisherman. Slow, clear, shallow water, with all the classic mayfly hatches that trumpet the spring season. The water required nearly perfect casts on long light tippets, using fly imitations that had to be as realistic as possible. It was frustrating at times, but those waters and those selective trout really helped me to hone my skills. It was here that I learned to really understand how trout think, how water currents work on a fly line, and the drift of a fly. These experiences taught me the meaning of the word *patient*.

Wild trout country, Katahdin Stream, Maine

Lake and Mount Chocorua, New Hampshire

Mount Katahdin reflected in backcountry lake, Maine

I caught my first steelhead on the lower Brule where it empties into Lake Superior, after three years of trying. My tenacity had finally gained the notice and the respect of the local fishermen who recognized me from previous years. They took me under their wing, told me how to rig my fly rod to detect the very subtle strikes, where to look along discrete watery seams in the river, why the trout would be in those locations, and what flies to use.

The fight of a steelhead is always memorable, whether novice or grizzled veteran. This one hit and immediately exploded into a long run. I followed her course, keeping the line tense, but letting her have her way. Whenever she stopped pulling, I pulled. Over the course of our fight, time stood

Trout coming up to take
Royal Wulff fly

Fly casting on Battenkill
River, Vermont

still. Again and again, she made flight and I coaxed her closer, a dance of man and fish like I had never experienced before.

When her belly finally hit the shallow gravel, I knew I had her. She made one last valiant flight, but she was in my sights now, and I knew I had the upper hand. Exhausted and shaking, I somehow landed her. She was silver and crimson, fresh up out of the waters of Lake Superior. I removed the hook and sat back on my haunches to look at her. She was a large 9-pound hen with a

The perfect cast

Wild trout are too precious to catch only once.

Dogwood blooms trumpet in the spring fly-fishing season.

wide crimson band along her sides, heavily muscled and impossibly strong. Magnificent. I released the hook, gently cradling her quivering body in my ice-numbed hands, still in a state of awe at what I had done. I often wonder if I actually intended to release her. Maybe I did. At any rate, no one had told me to tail her.

I lost another even larger steelhead that week. In my memory, it probably went 14 pounds. Way too large to land in such a small river as the Brule. I was hooked. I was a steelhead fisherman for real from that week forward.

I miss the Brule. One of these days I will go home again.

A NEW YORK STATE OF MIND

Serious anglers can cast back as far as ancient Scotland and Izaak Walton's *Compleat Angler* to find the beginnings of the sport of fly fishing. Most of us can readily point to where the sport took hold in the United States—in an unassuming stream, of deep pools full of possibilities, fed by cold, clear springs. The Beaverkill. In my early days as a fly fisherman, I knew it only as the legend that it was. I had read everything there was to read on the subject, but I never made the pilgrimage east from my native Wisconsin spring creeks to ply its waters. My eyes were firmly set on western rivers. Though I eventually came east to find the river and fall under its spell, it

Orvis trout reel

Cool, misty morning stream

Forest detail—princess pine and moss

was my good friend, the noted writer and outdoorsman Tom Rosenbauer, who really opened my eyes to its secrets.

Just to speak the name Beaverkill is to evoke the history and the romance of the sport. It is a land made famous by Theodore Gordon, who wrote articles on the art of fishing with a dry fly for the *Fishing Gazette* in the 1890s. Many view the rivers of the Catskills—the Neversink, the Beaverkill, Esopus, Delaware, Willowemoc, and Schoharie—as a world of quaint streams and nostalgic beginnings. I prefer to think of them as they were in the late 1800s—a hotbed of innovation and idealism—where some of the country's first conservationists banded together to

*Red maple along an
Adirondack river, New York*

Fall colors on a Catskill river, New York

save streams from overfishing, where Charles Orvis, the inventor of the modern fly reel, tested reels, and where many well-known anglers developed new fly patterns specifically for these famous waters.

Every time I get the opportunity to step into one of these rivers, I feel that history. I sense the energy that drove these men to follow the passion of these waters. Whenever I am on these waters, I feel like it is my first day fishing. Every morning is new and every day is filled with possibilities.

I am not thinking of these earlier legendary figures. True, I work hard to match the historically significant and traditional flies that originated on these famous rivers. I have

Brook trout fall spawning colors

Blazing fall colors on Adirondack brook trout pond

Cascades on small stream in upstate New York

spent every spring for many years following that parade of spring hatches, starting with the Quill Gordons, the Hendricksons and Red Quills, March Browns, Light Cahills, Green Drakes, Blue Winged Olives. I feel the impulse to wear a bit of tweed at times and to tuck a flask into my vest pocket.

As someone who has spent his life designing new and better fishing equipment—faster rods, better reels, innovative waders—I find that on this stream my mind soon wanders to the possibilities. What is a better way to wade the slippery rocks, an easier way to cast a tight loop, a smarter way to retrieve my line? My heart may pound harder and faster on the big waters of the

Evening light on pond in Maine

West, and I may daydream a little more on the quieter streams of the Mid-South. Here, where it all began, my mind is sharp. Every outline is vivid, every cast the promise of a new beginning.

On these Catskill rivers I learned what those legendary men knew. Those men who designed the fly patterns that we still tie today, who invented new ways to fly fish and waxed poetic about

Brown trout

Small stream in the Catskills, New York

the streams—that there are places in the world that exist to inspire the mind, to rejuvenate the soul, and to instill passion in our hearts.

Don't tell me these founding rivers are quaint and nostalgic, best seen in the rearview mirror on our way to bigger and faster streams. Don't tell me that I am getting older either. On this day in May, the world is new, and we are as young as the springs that run to meet us. All of it is just a state of mind. In this case, a New York state of mind.

OPENING DAY ON THE FIREHOLE

For several years, we lived in Montana, and I managed a fly shop near Yellowstone National Park. Every spring, a good friend of mine named Lee Watson and I spent opening day on the Firehole River.

The Firehole was not opened for fishing until late in May. Often it took that long to ensure the snow was gone and the park staff ready to deal with another year of fishers and

Early morning mist on an Adirondack lake, New York

tourists. The mood of the river is always unpredictable that time of year. Add to the mix of weather and river conditions, the billowing, rising sulfur fumes from the many thermal features along the stream, protective elk and bison mamas, hungry bears, snowflakes in the air, and a hint of the lingering winter still present in the deep shadows, and the picture starts to take shape.

I can honestly say I don't remember an opening day on the Firehole when the sun was shining, the weather warm, or when the wind wasn't blowing some sort of moisture in our faces. Somehow that made those days even more special. There is something about dealing with harsh natural elements that etches a memory deeply into your psyche. Maybe it has to do with some long-forgotten survival instinct.

West Branch Ausable River, western New York

Branch Ausable River, New York

Being from other places, we knew that in late May the weather was warm and the sun gentle where friends and family lived. While their gardens were starting to grow, we were still stepping over piles of snow on our way to the stream, but in our heart of hearts, we knew we were the lucky ones. They didn't have the Firehole River and Yellowstone National Park in their backyards.

Lee and I had sacred traditions that were mandatory when fishing that first day on the river. Where we got these traditions, I am still not sure. I think they came from some deep place in Lee's creatively different mind.

Horseshoe Bend of Firehole River, Yellowstone National Park

I guess the rituals had to do with honoring the past gods and legends of fly-fishing lore. We had to wear our tweed jackets, and sensible hats were forbidden in favor of matching tweed caps. Dame Juliana would have it no other way. We fished our bamboo rods, and used only specifically tied English dry flies, even though we knew that there would be no surface hatches, much less fish feeding on the surface. On English chalk streams, you are not allowed to fish any other way, and so it was. Somehow we still managed to catch a few early rainbows and an occasional brown trout.

Lunches were always special. Lee brought the little stove that he used during guiding season to treat his guests to superb meals on the river. I was always his first client of the year. Lee had a knack for making wonderful streamside lunches. There was always hot coffee, special silver cups that were served half full in the style of afternoon English tea. At the end of the meal, the same

Cow elk chasing away young bull, late summer, Firehole River

Protective bison mama, Firehole River

Releasing brown trout on Firehole River

Misty morning light, Firehole River, Yellowstone National Park

*Landing a wild brown trout on the Yellowstone
River, Paradise Valley, Montana*

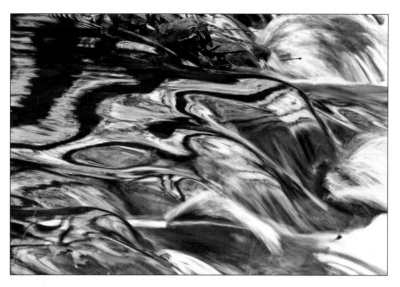

cups were filled, again just halfway, but this time with the finest single-malt scotch. We both kept a silver flask in our vests to keep the afternoon chill away.

Opening days are always special. You only get so many in your life. I still think of those harsh opening days on the Firehole every time I take a wee bit of the single malt. It seems to help free my mind so that I can think more creatively like my good friend Mr. Watson.

Rapidan River reflections—Virginia

Trout on Rapidan River over fall leaf detritus

Stream detail

First light, New England pond

Passing storm in Paradise Valley, Montana

Scouting for rising trout, Railroad Ranch Section of Henry's Fork River, Idaho

South Platte River canyon, Colorado

Tuolumne River, high-country meadows, Yosemite

PART TWO

The Living River

It is late fall. The aspens in the high country of the Wind River Range have already lost their leaves. The sunlight has changed significantly, and the days are much shorter. Air temperatures drop below freezing every night now. There have been brief snow flurries here in the meadows and real snows in the higher elevations for the past month. Spawning has begun for the trout in the upper Green River. Females have chosen spawning grounds. The males are in their full blaze of fall spawning colors. They are fighting for supremacy to mate with the fertile females. The largest male, vigorous and in his prime, will win out over the others. Aggressive young males hover close by and

Female cutthroat trout in shallow water near spawning site

challenge the dominant male constantly. There is a good chance they will be able to sow their milt over the eggs even if they lose the fight for the female. This is nature's way of ensuring diversity within the population. In time, these younger males will take their turn as the strongest mate.

The female trout chooses her spawning site with considerable care. Moving water is imperative. Water temperature and depth are also critical factors. Another critical factor is the size and location of gravel. Spawning gravel has to be within a specific size range for any real success to occur. There are several factors that come into play. First, it has to be small enough for the female trout to move it with her tail. If it is too small, the eggs will not be able to settle within the spaces between the pebbles and could potentially wash away during flooding, they are more available to predation, and once hatched there is not enough protective cover. If the gravel is too large, she may not be able to move the gravel effectively. The chance of silt piling deep within the crevices of the larger stones or pebbles is much greater, and it may be more difficult for the eggs to get enough of the free-flowing oxygen that is essential to their survival.

There is much competition for the best spawning beds. The female stations herself over her chosen bed until the time is right. The strongest male guards the bed and the female. She lies on her side and flaps her tail up and down feverishly to open a shallow hollow in the

Headwater spawning stream

Headwaters of Maroon Creek tributary of the Roaring Fork, first light, Maroon Bells, Aspen, Colorado

gravel. Once the bed is complete, the male moves next to the female and their bodies quiver in unison. The female releases eggs while the male releases his milt.

Then the female moves upstream and opens up another shallow area in the gravel directly above the first bed. In the process, she covers the first bed with gravel to protect the eggs. She and the male will repeat the same process until the female has released all of her eggs. The size and age of the female as well as the quality and size of the spawning beds will determine the number of eggs laid and the number of beds that are made.

This process leaves the female trout spent and exhausted. She may or

Headwaters, Sandy Stream Pond and Mount Katahdin, Maine

Trout stacking up as spawning time nears

may not survive through the coming winter. Age, physical condition, and water conditions will all be contributing factors in her ability to survive for another season.

The eggs that have been left behind will hatch on their own in forty to ninety days, depending on water temperatures. The warmer the water, the faster the eggs will hatch. Optimum water temperatures of 50–52 degrees will see 95 percent of the eggs hatch in forty-four days or so. Many of the same variables that determine the female's future apply to egg survival.

The alevin hatch with egg sacs intact, and will live in the gravel substrate for another four to six weeks, nourished by their sacs. After that, they are entirely on their own to forage for food. At this point they emerge as fry from the gravel substrate. The fry leave the protective home of the substrate to swim freely. Within days, the stream will be filled with thousands of tiny free-swimming fry, less than 1 inch in length. This phenomenon will not go unnoticed. It is at this

Small trout spawning stream in Wind River Range

Trout near spawning time

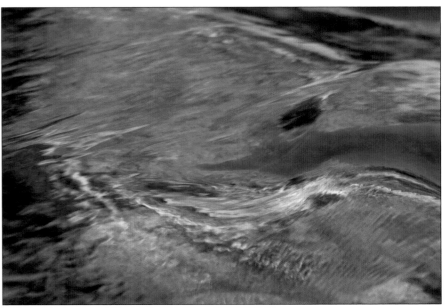

As river music plays, the fall spawning dance begins.

River currents, Swift River, New Hampshire

Sunlit side pool, a perfect home for fingerling trout

time the tiny trout become most vulnerable. They will become easy prey for the larger members of their own species, as well as kingfishers, herons, ospreys, otters, raccoons, and others. Of the thousands of fry that emerge from the spawning beds, only a small percentage will grow large enough to become fingerlings. The 1- to 4-inch fingerlings now start to resemble mature trout.

They develop parr marks that help to give them a natural camouflage. They will keep these marks through the first year.

Fingerlings live on the edges of streams in the little rock eddies and among the detritus. They feed on plankton to begin, but soon start feeding on tiny insects, larva, and pupae. By the end of the first summer, the surviving fingerlings will have reached 4–5 inches in length. Survival rates are extremely low, 1–3 percent after the first year.

At a year old, the young trout become smolts. A transformation occurs as they ready to move from their natal stream into the larger, deeper, more enriched waters downstream. Here, they will find more protection, more food opportunities, and more danger.

At this point only the smartest, strongest, and swiftest trout survive. They are now part of the greater ecosystem. They will have to fight for positions within the stream that offer easy opportunities for food and protection from predators. They begin to zero in on the insects that live in the stream and become predators to smaller fish, including the next generation of fry and fingerling trout. The rule of survival in this watery world is simple; the bigger morsels you eat,

Mountain brook trout stream, Virginia

*Boulder River,
Montana*

the faster and larger you grow. Only the biggest, strongest, smartest, and most aggressive will take part in creation of future generations.

HOME IS WHERE THE TROUT ARE

In our fast-paced world, the concept of the home stream may be charming, but in practical terms, unrealistic for many of us. Careers take us many places over the course of our lives, and fewer of us have the luxury of that one home place, but ask a fisherman about his home stream,

Riffles—Gallatin River, Montana

and he will have a ready answer. Many fishers cast back in time to their first stream to name their home stream. That is my standard reply. Others name the stream that has made the biggest impact on them. Some have vacation homes near a particular river. That is their home stream. My work has taken me to live in Montana, Maine, Vermont, and Virginia. Each time, my place

Gallatin River, Montana

Pocket water on
the Gallatin River,
Montana

Our stream allies, dragonflies are like little Apache helicopters that zero in on mosquitoes and no-see-ums.

Fall colors on Saco River,
New Hampshire

Blue Ridge
Mountain stream

Cabin on the Magalloway River, Maine

there was not complete until I found a piece of river to call my own. I am not sure they can honestly be called my home waters. I do know that without them, I could not feel at home.

When we lived in Montana, I considered the Gallatin my home river. The Gallatin is a place of high-country meadows, shaded canyons, endless riffles, and willing fish. Elk can often be seen grazing nearby, and the occasional bear comes ambling through. I taught my children to fish there. I still miss it and try to fish it at least once every year.

Then there is opening day on the Firehole River in Yellowstone National Park: fishing with bamboo rods, wearing tweed jackets, having lunch along the bank, often in snow squalls, drinking single-malt scotch from silver flasks to take away the chill. It's not my home river, perhaps, but it holds a very special place in my heart.

We spent many years living in Maine. I developed fly-fishing products for L.L. Bean. It was my job to fly fish. People told me all the time I had the best job in the world. It is very possible I did. After living in the heart of western trout country in Montana, it took me a while to really adapt to the streams and rivers of the northeast. The northeastern rivers are so different from the wide open brawling rivers of the West, even the smaller western streams.

Fly fishermen,
South Holston
River, Tennessee,
before release

Eastern rivers and streams have a close, intimate feel. The horizons are near, their pathways narrow. In time, I began to fall in love with many of the trout waters of New England. Fishing the truly wild Magalloway with its native brook trout and landlocked salmon takes you back in time. The backwoods cabins, often without electricity, are nearly the same as they were a hundred years ago, the fishing experience much the same also.

I fondly remember days of fishing Grand Lake Stream with good friend Macauley Lord in the days when we ran the Bean Fly-Fishing Schools up there. It is a short bit of river, or more appropriately a stream. It leaves Grand Lake and flows approximately 4 miles before dumping into Bass Lake, but those few miles of stream are magical and full of large wild trout.

Maybe the closest thing to a western river is the West Branch of the Penobscot below the dam. It flows east and winds through white pines and second-growth timber toward the Atlantic

Small New Hampshire stream

Swift River Fall,
New Hampshire

Ocean. It is large enough, and its rapids big enough, to make it a dangerous river to wade. It also holds large trout and is wide enough to offer fly-casting room like a big western river.

Often on weekends or days off, I would work in Bill Hunter's famous little fly shop in New Boston, New Hampshire. Bill is a pro's pro. Bill turned me on to some of the best little streams in New Hampshire and how to fish them. He gave me the keys to the real magic of eastern streams.

The rainbow of colors of river music

Little white-tailed buck thinks he is camouflaged in streamside thicket

There are several little rivers in northern New Hampshire that became favorites because of the cold clear waters and bright, wild trout. The Ammonoosuc, the Pemigewasset, the Zealand, the Swift, and upper Saco were my favorite spring and fall rivers. They offer enough room to fly cast, they are shallow enough to wade, and they are classic pocket-water rivers. In the fall, they are spectacular. The fall colors are the best I have found anywhere in the world.

I spent a few years in Vermont. I was the head of fly-fishing product development for Orvis there. Again, my job was to fly fish. Our offices were close to the famous Battenkill River. We rented a house just a quarter mile off the river, near the border where the river flowed into New York State. The Battenkill became my home water for those years. I have to say the Battenkill valley is one of my favorite places anywhere. It is the perfect setting for a classic trout stream. Even though the river is very fishable, the fishing is anything but easy. My good friend from Orvis, Jim Logan, head of Orvis rod manufacturing, lives on the river and in his spare time makes beautiful handcrafted wooden drift boats that he uses on the river three or four nights a week during fishing season.

Wild Katahdin Stream, Baxter State Park, Maine

Jim knows the river very well, even has names for some of the larger brown trout he has caught a few times. He taught me a lot about the fishing on this wonderful, historic little river. I would have eventually found the best places to fish and the right flies to use, but Jim's guidance

Katahdin Stream, Maine

*Wild northern
Maine stream*

*Dogwood morning
light along Rapidan
River, Virginia*

and friendship made all of it much more worthwhile. The Battenkill is really his home river. I borrowed it only for a short while, but I am glad I had the opportunity.

We live in Virginia now. Again, it took me a while to locate and get to know the best rivers and streams. We are tucked up against the Blue Ridge Mountains. There are literally dozens of delightful trout streams running out of these old worn-down mountains. The trout fishing here is actually better than most of the fishing I found in New England. The rivers are more fertile, the fishing seasons go year-round. Some of the best fishing can be had in the winter months of December through February. The spring and fall seasons last for a full three months each.

River reflection and pink dogwood, Virginia

Male Carolina wren singing love songs on early spring morning along Virginia stream

Tumbling Blue Ridge Mountain stream

There is a parade of pastel flowering trees and shrubs along the streams from March through May. In the fall, the weather stays warm well into December, and the fall colors hang around until mid-November. For a boy who grew up in the cold winters of Wisconsin, Montana, and Maine, the long warm seasons of Virginia are precious.

I have one very special stream among this abundance. Every day on the stream is like visiting a jewel box, reflected sunlight dappled on the varied greens of summer and the rippling vibrant oranges and yellows of fall, and, best of all, pools of gem-colored brook trout, friendly and eager. I promised my friend Dargan, who shared it with me, that I wouldn't tell its name. The water temperatures produce nice hatches, and the fish are strong and energized. As I get older, this little river makes me feel the same way.

SPRING CREEKS I HAVE KNOWN

Spring creeks I have known—most are like beautiful, sophisticated women or exotic sports cars or fine wine. They are surpassingly tempting, seemingly unapproachable, wildly temperamental, and unusually expensive. Once you unlock their mystery and nuance, they are simply amazing.

Merced River, California

Morning light,
Armstrong Spring
Creek, Montana

Fly fishermen on
Armstrong Spring Creek,
Montana

At least that is how I like to think of them.

I have fished spring creeks in many places around the world. I have had the pleasure and good fortune to spend unhurried days casting dry flies over the educated and wary trout along England's rivers Test and Itchen. To work my way through those murky bottom beats of long-held private waters is like going back in time. I am treading waters that in the past were open only to kings and lords and princes. Today, even money may not be enough to get you on these

Morning light, DePuy Spring Creek, Montana

rivers—one must be invited to come and spend your money to fish for a day or weekend. The traditions here are as old as the sport of fly fishing itself. It was quite enjoyable, I must say, old chap.

The limestone spring creeks of Pennsylvania are almost as close as you will get to those British classics. Unlike the British versions, which are fairly long, these are rather diminutive, but they are filled with beautiful browns and rainbows. I have spent many days on the limestone spring creeks of south-central Pennsylvania. It was nice of my daughter to choose a college near that part of the world.

Without question, my favorite spring creeks reside in Paradise Valley in Montana. Armstrong, DePuy, and Nelson Spring creeks are the jewels of Paradise Valley. They surround the Yellowstone River in the upper end of the valley.

Fly fishing in Armstrong Spring Creek, Montana

Aquatic vegetation on Pennsylvania spring creek

Stormy afternoon—DePuy Spring Creek; Montana

Spring creek sunrise, Montana

Paradise is a fitting name for this magnificent wide valley with the Yellowstone River running through it for the entire length of the valley. Rich, fertile bottomlands gently slope down to the river on both sides. Framed in by the Absarokas on the east and the Gallatin Range on the west, it is the quintessential western landscape.

DePuy is essentially the lower portion of Armstrong before it empties into the west side of the Yellowstone. Nelson sits nearly directly across from Armstrong on the eastern side of the river. While there are similarities, all three waters are different. All are worth the time and money to get to know.

These are classic dry fly waters. Consistent water temperatures and flows mean an abundance of insect life nearly year-round and a healthy population of large wild trout. While they are expensive and require reservations, they only allow a handful of rods on the river each day. So you have plenty of room to fish without the anxiety of someone trying to move you out of that great spot you just found.

It is truly a paradise for a fly fisher.

Trout stacked in cool waters of natural spring

Evening Light—
DePuy Spring
Creek, Montana

Spring creeks can be extremely difficult, or magical, depending on your skill level, the time of day, and the season. You will need to make precise casts, with long, thin leaders, with tiny dry flies and nymphs size 20 and smaller. Oh, and you better factor the wind into those precise casts. This is Montana, and this is a wide and open valley. Wind in Montana is a little like a heartbeat. If it stops, you feel some anxiety and wonder if the world just stood still.

That is only the beginning. Looking closely into these waters, you see that they are filled with a great deal of aquatic vegetation. This vegetation changes the game in a major way. The

Nelson Spring Creek, Paradise Valley,
Montana; Releasing a western spring
creek rainbow trout

Landing rainbow trout on DePuy Spring Creek

smooth, mellow speed of the glass-clear water is affected by the weed layers from top to bottom and from side to side within the stream. The weeds cause multiple seams within the stream, and different water speeds at the same time. On the surface, it looks fairly simple to make a 25-foot cast to a rising trout just across and upstream. In reality, there are probably seven different water seams and water speeds between you and that large rainbow.

So while you may have made the precisely perfect cast and landed the fly exactly in the right place 24 inches above the trout's nose, your 14-foot leader is being wiggled into unimaginable *Zs* formed by all the different water speeds across the many seams. Within moments of landing in the precise spot, your fly begins to dance and race from the pull of that doggone leader.

This is where the game gets interesting for some individuals and frustrating for others. It seems the biggest and smartest fish already know the game. They take up residence in the hardest

DePuy
Spring Creek,
Montana

Concentration is needed to follow your tiny flies on clear spring creeks.

places to reach, making it very difficult to successfully fool them with an imitation. They see literally thousands of minute insects float by them every day in gin-clear water. Your imitation, if not the exact size, color, and movement, will be detected in a heartbeat. In this match of skill and wiles, the fish scores a point.

This is the moment that defines a man's character. Is it "game on" or "game over"?

That is the magic of these places. No matter the outcome, just playing the game in these fertile fly-

Brown trout on Armstrong
Spring Creek, Montana

Nelson Spring Creek,
Paradise Valley, Montana

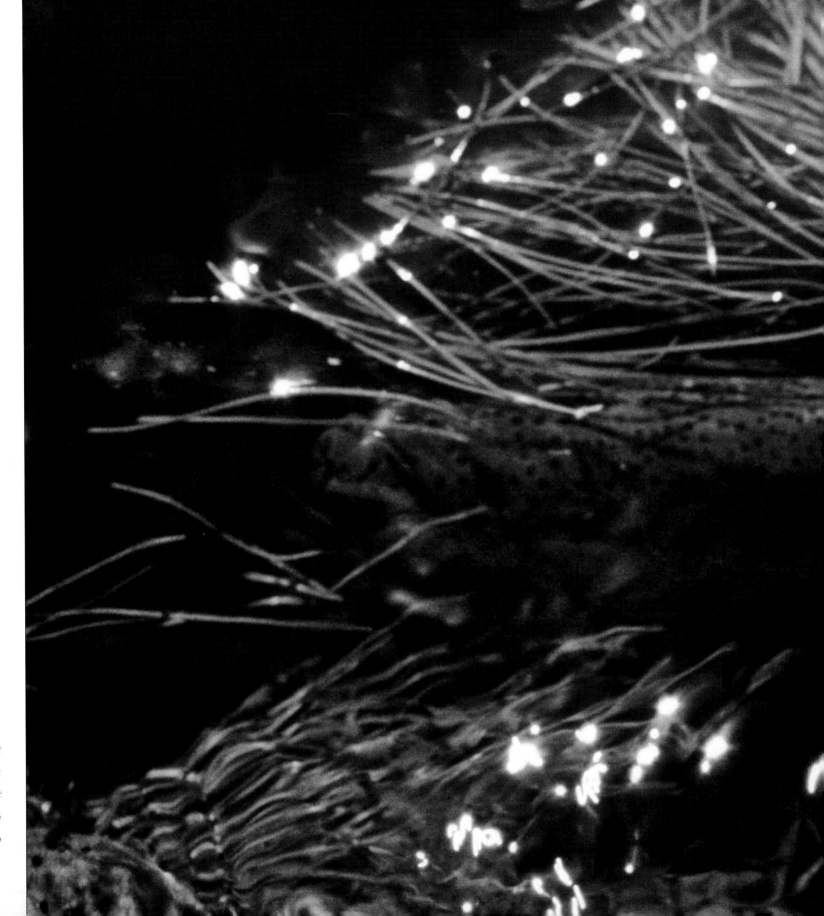

Spring creek trout hidden in stream grasses making it nearly impossible to catch

DePuy
Spring Creek,
Montana

fishing nirvanas sweeps your mind from every care and worry. For one afternoon, it is just you and the fish. Expensive? For sure. Priceless? You bet.

THE PERFECT RIVER: ROCK CREEK

I know nearly every state has at least one Rock Creek. In my mind, none compare to Rock Creek in western Montana. This one is the quintessential small western trout water. I took

82

my first big rainbow on Rock Creek my first summer out of high school. It weighed in at 3 pounds—at the time the biggest trout I had ever caught.

I had departed, with some trepidation, right after high school graduation, armed for the West with an old truck, a single fiberglass fly rod, and a hundred bucks. I was in search of mountains, adventure, and wild trout. I had heard of Rock Creek, how and from whom I can no longer recall. As soon as I got to Montana, I was determined to fish it.

Trout shadow—Rock Creek, Montana

Fly fishing Rock Creek, Montana

The drive into Rock Creek canyon is like driving back in time. The narrow road runs alongside the wandering creek, drawing you back farther and farther until you hardly know where you are. The river itself calls to you at every turn. With its shallow riffles, provocative channels and pools, and fast runs, every foot of 30 miles calls out *"fish me."*

A series of rises drew my attention to a particular bend in the river. I pulled over and got out my rod. A hatch of medium-sized light mayflies was coming off the water. This was a good sign. I had recently learned to tie a pretty decent Light Cahill, and I considered it my lucky fly. I pulled one out of my fly box. It was a good match for the hatching mayflies. I worked my way into casting range, made a few bad casts, and then finally dropped the fly exactly where I wanted it, about 3 feet above that tantalizing rise.

Rainbow trout on Rock Creek, Montana

The drift was perfect. The fish took it in a flashy swirl like a smaller fish will often do. At first, I thought I had miscalculated its size, but then it leapt out of the water, 3 feet in the air. A huge rainbow. At that time in my trout-fishing life, I felt that I was living out one of those moments you only read about in *Outdoor Life* magazine. Somehow, I have a still-life photograph of that rainbow suspended in the air etched in my memory. The bright, large crimson stripe along its twisting side flank, the small dark spots along its upper back, the silver flash of

Middle section of Rock Creek, Montana

Afternoon light, Rock Creek, Montana

light, muscle, and wildness that only the image of a leaping wild rainbow trout can embed in one's memory. It resides in my mind, looking just like the paintings that would accompany the *Outdoor Life* article in the sixties.

I landed another half dozen beautiful rainbows that afternoon, none as large as the first, but all nice wild western rainbow trout. I only had two of my Light Cahills. I soon lost the first fly to another fish, but the second fly kept me going through most of the hatch. Once I lost it, my day was over. The hatch was over, the feeding frenzy enough to satisfy the wild fish and a young, half-frenzied fly fisherman.

Rock Creek winds for 55 miles in a northwesterly direction just east of Missoula, Montana, before dumping into the Clark Fork. In its upper reaches, it is brook trout water. As feeder

Golden dragonfly waiting for the sun to warm his wings to fly

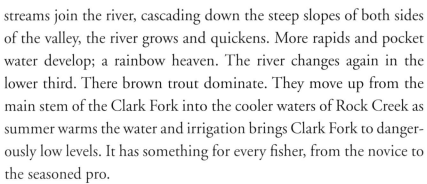

Red columbine along stream in Montana

Damselfly

streams join the river, cascading down the steep slopes of both sides of the valley, the river grows and quickens. More rapids and pocket water develop; a rainbow heaven. The river changes again in the lower third. There brown trout dominate. They move up from the main stem of the Clark Fork into the cooler waters of Rock Creek as summer warms the water and irrigation brings Clark Fork to dangerously low levels. It has something for every fisher, from the novice to the seasoned pro.

I choose not to calculate how many years ago that first day on Rock Creek was. While the river has not changed appreciably, it has suffered somewhat from the stresses of its abundance. Fishers flock to its banks for the summer salmon fly hatch as well as for the autumn spawning runs. Whirling disease has also been found in the stream.

We really need to protect these little jewels like Rock Creek. Every generation deserves the right to fish splendid little wild rivers for wild trout.

NO BIG DEAL

Winters are brutal in Montana. We lived at close to 7,000 feet in elevation. The snows and cold winds came quickly in the fall and lasted for six solid months. That was just the way things were. No big deal. One winter we moved from one rental house to another and didn't realize we had a 6-foot-high wooden fence around the yard until late April. The snow on the level ground was somewhere between 10 and 12 feet most of the winter.

The temperatures were every bit as bad. Every January we would have two to three weeks of nighttime temperatures that would drop down to 50 degrees below zero. Daytime highs

Canoe country, northern Maine

River music kaleidoscope

were around 30 below. No big deal. I remember leaving for the fly shop very clearly one spring Thursday morning. It was April 28. I put on only a vest over my shirt—it seemed like a nice, sunny spring morning. As I left the house, I looked at the outside thermometer. It was 28 degrees below zero. I didn't even flinch, nor did I feel the need to put on more clothes. No big deal.

The streets in West Yellowstone were not plowed, but rather groomed and packed for the use of the snowmobiles. Our children followed paths in the snow that were forged by intrepid

*Upper
Ammonoosuc River,
New Hampshire*

Wild river, Baxter State Park, Maine

others to get to school. Often these paths led to someone's back door and then out the front door. Neighbors were used to the comings and goings. No big deal. Easter-egg hunts took place in 30-foot snow banks, and Easter bonnets were replaced with wool caps and fuzzy bunny ears. Children were as likely to play on the roof of the house as in the backyard—there was no real distinction between solid earth and clouds of snow. The world was white. No big deal.

The days were short and the nights were long while we sat in front of the fire dreaming of open rivers. Stories of fish fought and fish won, stories of picnic days and starry evenings, kept us warm with hope. We skied and snowshoed and made the best of it with big pots of moose stew and venison chili, but the cold always insinuated itself into our dreams. Many days, it seemed that the summer would never come. Even in paradise, things aren't always rosy. Reminder to self: When chasing your dreams, keep in the back of your mind that the grass isn't always greener on the other side of the daydream.

I wouldn't trade those days for anything. While we worked hard and dealt with long, cold winters, we also spent every waking minute of summer and fall exploring

Stream detail

Rounded granite and maple leaf; River currents

the mountains, rivers, and streams in this wonderful part of America. It has become part of the weft and the warp in the fabric that has become our life. Those colors are rich and vibrant and deeply woven into our beings. The friends we made and the experiences shared made our lives richer and made us better people. Looking back on those times from a great distance, it seems that even the snows and the cold carry a rosy pink glow.

Maroon Bells—Rocky Mountain high

PART THREE

Rivers of Trout, Rivers of Time

It is mid-summer. The high-country meadows are lush. Wildflowers dot the green carpet of grasses and low scrub along the river. The winds are warm. The sun sprays its radiant energy across everything in the valley for long hours each day. Life is good.

Here in the high country, life has to flourish in the summer months. Summer is short up here. The intensity of growth is magnified by the shortness of the season. Fall will come all too soon, followed quickly and harshly by the long winter months.

Upper Green River, Square Top Mountain, Wind River Range, Wyoming

Insect life in the river is at its peak. The sun and warming water temperatures have flipped the switch to optimum for inhabitants of the upper Green River. Mayfly larva hatch from the sediment in the side eddies of the long slick of slower water. They mature quickly and soon emerge as nymphs, swimming erratically to the surface of the river to become duns.

As they work to shuck their nymphal hulls at the surface of the water, trout take notice. The mayflies are easy prey at this time. The water temperature is perfect, and thousands of nymphs are making their way to the watery surface. The hatch is on.

Fly fishing
Green
River Lake,
Wyoming

As in virtually everything in nature, there is a connectedness, a rhythm, a cadence between species, between predator and prey. It is a primal dance that keeps everything in balance. The perfect conditions for mayflies to hatch and escape the river to mate in an aerial dance high above the river currents are also the perfect conditions for the trout to be most active and most aggressive in search of food.

Wild western cutthroat trout rising to fly

*Evening hatch, Railroad
Ranch, Henry's Fork,
Idaho*

*Mayfly on fly
patch*

The hatch is on.

The water surface is alive with watery swirls and boils. Trout of all sizes are feeding on the vulnerable nymphs struggling in the meniscus of the surface film. As the mayflies wiggle out of their armored suits, they turn into delicate flying duns with transparent wings. From a distance, they look like dozens of miniature fairies ascending into the trees along the river.

In reality it is a numbers game. Similar to the alevin trout that emerge from the gravel spawning beds into the stream, thousands of mayfly nymphs must emerge for a handful to escape to carry on the mating dance.

For the fly fisher, the frenzy of activity quickens the pulse. Frantic, ecstatic mayflies and the swirl of rising trout draw us into the dance. We are predators, too. We are by nature energized.

Swirl as trout
takes a fly

Stonefly nymphal shucks on streamside rock

and fascinated by the scene. Somehow we can also see beyond it, as all our senses are engaged in understanding the immense beauty of the moment.

The rhythmic dance of mating mayflies hovering over the river. Sweet warm evening breezes. The smell of earth, of summer wildflowers, the song of the whippoorwill in the distance. It is our ability to take all this in that separates us from all other species. We see the beauty and passion of the moment, knowing that playing out before us is a Shakespearean tragedy.

Fly casting for rising trout »

These mayflies have just this one dance, this one night. Then it is over. In the morning, their wings will have turned translucent, and the river eddies will be covered with their spent bodies.

Most mayfly males will only live for twenty-four hours after they emerge and turn into duns. The females will live for a few more days. In the days to come, they will descend back to the river to deposit their eggs. Dancing above the water surface like puppets on an invisible string, the females break the water's surface to deposit their tiny clutch of eggs. The cluster of eggs is held together by a sticky membrane that is heavier than water and quickly sinks to the bottom of the river. The dance is complete; the cycle begins again.

These are the moments that make up the fly fisher's world. We love the unfurling curve of the fly line above the water, the dappled, delicate landing of the imitation fly as it touches the water surface. At this moment, the world of the trout is our world. We melt into crystal-clear waters on a warm summer eve, to cast a fly, see the swirl, feel the tug, and ultimately to release the splendid, wild jewel of magic called trout.

Searching for the right fly

Trying to match the hatch, Railroad Ranch, Henry's Fork, Idaho

Fishing the Boulder River, Montana

The fisher's relationship with the trout and the waters where they live is a complex one. This fish, these rivers, bring out everything that is remarkable about being human. Predator and prey. The hunt and the chase. The passing of time and the heart-stopping beauty.

This is why our time on trout water is so precious. We know these are the moments that make up our own fragile life, and the short existence on this planet we call home.

THE FISHBOWL

The wilderness of Yellowstone National Park is something of an enigma. While it has been set aside as a natural, wild preserve for elk, bison, deer, and wild trout, it sometimes feels more like a giant fishbowl. Millions of people visit every year, poking and prodding at the glass walls, peering at the intimate lives of the citizens within, but never really understanding exactly what they are seeing. Maybe that's because most of them never wander more than 70 feet from their car.

Beautiful Yellowstone River cutthroat trout

Bugling bull elk ready to start fall rut, Firehole River

Most of the tourist activity comes during the four months between June and September. Like the elk, we look forward to October. The bison don't seem to care.

   This phenomenon has both good and bad side effects. The bad side, of course, is that it has clogged up the roadways to a point that it is sometimes nearly impossible to get from one side

Lazy summer afternoon on the Yellowstone River, Paradise Valley, Montana

of the park to another. On the positive side, most of the park, once you are a few hundred yards from the roads, is essentially real wilderness.

The rivers and streams of Yellowstone are still managed for wild trout. Yellowstone waters provide some of the most important headwaters in the West. Yes, there are more fly fishers than ever fishing these streams. The fishing is still pretty good and the experience still worth the effort. The rivers are still cold, clear, and essentially unchanged since the end of the last Ice Age. Yellowstone at its finest represents a wonderfully eclectic mix of river types.

Bison, Yellowstone National Park

The Yellowstone River exits Yellowstone Lake in the heart of the park as a full-blown, wide, classic western river. Its crystal-clear waters offer a steady flow of depth and temperatures all during the open season. This produces a rich, abundant insect life, and in turn, a rich, healthy population of native Yellowstone cutthroat trout.

Unfortunately, things are not always what they seem, or perhaps what they should be. Lake trout that were planted in Yellowstone Lake many years ago have started to push native cutthroat out of their normal range and threaten to severely weaken the native population. The Yellowstone Lake cutthroat trout population has declined to less than 10 percent of its historic number

Bull elk, afternoon siesta at Slough Creek meadows

*Fly fishing below
Gibbon Falls,
Yellowstone
National Park*

Landing trout at base of Gibbon Falls, Yellowstone National Park

while the lake trout population has continued to increase. The loss of Yellowstone cutthroat trout has significant effects on the entire Yellowstone ecosystem. In fact, there currently are more than fifteen major western waters where lake trout have outgrown their forage or have negatively impacted native species. Yellowstone Lake is the most severely impacted. The job of fixing this is massive and controversial. Several of the western states, along with the National Park Service, have initiated efforts to control lake trout numbers in their impacted waters but so far with only marginal success.

Far from being innocent observers on the outside of the fishbowl, man has interfered enough with the delicate balance of the Yellowstone fishery to endanger one of the most important and pure natural trout species in our American heritage.

DIVERGENT PATHS

I love the rivers and streams of Yellowstone country. Having lived there and guided there for several years, it is still like going home whenever we return. I have degrees in geology, river ecology, and business. Interesting combination, but somehow they have served me well. Each

Elephant Rock, Gibbon River, Yellowstone National Park

Yellowstone River
cutthroat trout

has played an important role in various parts of my work life. Each in their own way could have taken me in a number of directions. Somehow I always knew they would take me to exactly where I am now.

Two of my favorite rivers in the park are very different. Both eventually make their way to the Missouri River, but they take completely different paths to do so.

The Firehole River starts out in the west-central part of the park as a series of feeder streams and underground seepages and combines with a myriad of thermal discharges to form one of the most interesting rivers on earth. You literally can catch a 12-inch brown trout on certain stretches of the river and parboil it right there. It is amazing that trout can live so close to some of these thermal features that empty their boiling waters directly into the river.

The Firehole runs fairly shallow its entire length until it joins the Gibbon River at Madison Junction to form the headwaters of the Madison River inside the park. The substrate is volcanic. Of course, the entire Yellowstone basin is, but it is different than the Yellowstone River. The bottom is a series of hard volcanic ledges and small potholes that offer needed aeration and hiding places for trout and the insect population. It is wide enough and open in many areas. Its shallow water makes it the perfect wading stream to fly fish.

Of course there is always an asterisk; the reality is that fishing the Firehole can be difficult. The fish population is made up primarily of browns and rainbows, with the brown trout

Bull elk afternoon, Slough Creek meadows

making up a larger portion of the population in the lower, warmer parts of the river. Except for the upper stretches of the river, insect populations are somewhat sparse also. Because of the substrate, shallow depth, and harsh winters that build up bottom ice through much of the year, large areas of the river bottom are fairly devoid of the essential elements for insect life to take hold. So the trout never grow as large as one would imagine they should in the Firehole.

Even though it can be difficult, and there are not as many fish available, it is still a dream river for a fly fisher.

Big Yellowstone River brown trout

Slough Creek in the northeastern corner of the park is my other favorite. It is completely different than the Firehole. It starts out as several smaller streams rushing out of the Beartooth Plateau, draining south to join the Lamar River and then into the Yellowstone inside the park. In my early days of guiding, Slough Creek was just starting to become known to the greater fly-fishing world, but you could still spend a few days in the upper meadows without seeing a lot of fishers, and you could share the area with no one more than a little wildlife.

This has changed now in recent years. Slough Creek gets a tremendous amount of pressure every summer. I guess it should. It is a beautiful stream. Its three upper meadows are in spectacular country, wide open with the possibility of encountering a real live grizzly bear. Seeing these critters is no longer a personal aspiration of mine. I spent too many days up there guiding dudes from big cities who were fairly clueless about the dangers involved being too close to these unpredictable creatures. These days, I am happy to take a grizzly-free day on the stream. I am happy they are there, but I am sure they would agree that we are better off traveling in different spheres.

The native cutthroat trout are large, plentiful, reasonably easy to catch, and the water is very accessible. It is another dream scenario for a trout fisher. It is a place I still dream about when things here in the East are too close and oppressive.

Yellowstone River overlook, Paradise Valley, Montana

Guide trip, evening light, Yellowstone River, Montana

Grand Tetons reflected in morning light

STEELHEADED

I have always felt that steelhead got their name not because of the bright steel color they exhibit that time of year but because those of us that fish for them are steelheaded in our blind pursuit of this fish. We subject ourselves to the pain and numbness that is the trademark of this sport in our passionate chase of these wild and difficult-to-catch sea-run trout.

Steelheading is the toughest of sport. It is an all-out battle with the wind and the cold. Ice freezes your rod guides so that line can't slip through them. Fingers and hands are frozen and numb. The nose never stops running, and eyes water from the stinging winds. Ice crystals collect on eyelashes and beard. Remarkably, as long as your feet are in the river, they are warm—a small blessing that lasts only until you hit the shore.

Fly casting for trout on Leigh Lake in Grand Teton National Park

Fishing crystal-clear, shallow stream in Grand Teton National Park

It is a lonely week. Few, even the most diehard trout-fishing friends, want to freeze themselves into numbness to catch a handful of trout, even if they are huge and explode from the cold dark river waters like the gods of the deep that they are.

It gets worse. Steelheading requires persistence. Fishing for eight to ten hours a day for seven days straight may gain you the privilege of hooking one fish a day. With luck and skill, you may land four in a week. When you land one, the adrenaline of the fight warms you for hours afterward.

The rewards are as great as the effort you expend. Hooking, fighting, and eventually landing a bright, crimson-sided steelhead that weighs somewhere between 6 and 18 pounds is worth all the pain and freezing digits. After years of steelhead fishing, I can still feel every one of those fish in my hands. I remember the movement of the dark rivers, the

Releasing brown trout on Firehole River

Fly casting for rainbows

124

Young bull elk in Firehole River

icy cold, the exhilaration of landing, and the moment of releasing each and every one of those magnificent fish.

There is a moment of grace in the catching. Right before the steelhead is released, we are together in the stream, both breathing heavily, both having proven our toughness and our sinew in the pitch of battle. Sharing this moment, man and fish, brings me closer to my ancestral ties. It brings clarity to the rest of my life. The memory of this battle will keep me sane and balanced when the rigors of my other life threaten to throw me out of balance.

I am labeled one of those Steelhead Bums. Friends truly think I am crazy, but I know there is respect and a little awe behind the mocking tones.

High-country meadows— Lamar River Valley, Yellowstone National Park

Slough Creek trout in shallows after being released

Today it is the middle of February. The winds are whipping out of the north-northwest at a sustained 30 miles per hour. Or so reads the little gauge hanging on my wall. Even though the sun is out, the wind makes it miserable just to be outdoors. These days, I don't go after steelhead the way I once did. I live in Virginia, and I have come to enjoy the softness and delicacy of the Blue Ridge Mountain streams and their diminutive natives. At least that is my excuse. Today, with the snow flying and the wind threatening, I can't help but long for those days on the big water, where I tested my mettle against the wild instincts of silver monsters. I take rod in hand

and head to the stream to capture a shadow of that past, of frozen fingers and pitched battles, even if the biggest fish I catch today is a 10-inch native brook trout.

WHERE FLOWS THE UMPQUA

The North Umpqua is one of those rivers that pulled at my heartstrings from the first time I fished it. I am always a little torn between fishing a river and photographing it. I am an outdoor photographer by trade, but have not always been.

Golden aspens of early fall—upper Slough Creek meadows

Fly fishing for northwestern winter steelhead, Washington

The first time I fished the Umpqua, I was a product manager for a major retailer. My boss and I were visiting one of the vendors that provided us with flies for our stores and catalogs. He was an ardent fisherman, so our three days there were already mapped out—meetings all day Friday, and then fishing the Umpqua for the early fall steelhead run on Saturday and Sunday.

Brilliant fresh-run steelhead

Cascades on North Umpqua River, Oregon

*North Umpqua
River, Oregon*

The water was in beautiful condition, but a little low, so there were not a lot of fish in the river. They needed a new freshet to raise the water level a little and to get the fish moving into and up the river. The weather was perfect though: crisp autumn air, chilly mornings, and temperatures in the mid-60s in the afternoons.

Fishing for steelhead, North Umpqua River, Oregon

I am crazy about rivers and can find the positive in almost any river, but the North Umpqua really is special. I fell in love immediately. We were up at the crack of dawn Saturday morning. I wanted to be there to photograph the river in first light. My boss couldn't wait to get his line wet. I spent the first day alternating between fishing and photographing. I was almost intoxicated with the beauty of the river. It is hard to concentrate on both fishing and photography at the same time.

North Umpqua River volcanic rock structures

Fishing for steelhead on the Umpqua is not for novices. It is tough and technical. You have to know what you are doing to have any chance of catching, much less landing, one of these sea-run heart-stoppers. I had been a successful steelhead fisherman for years, but each river is different and presents a whole new set of problems to solve. This river topped any I had fished for degree of difficulty.

Steelhead fishing,
North Umpqua River,
Oregon

The two local fishermen who accompanied us were both very experienced and successful Umpqua fly fishermen. They were our guides for the weekend. They put us on the best water, gave us the best flies to use, and showed us the most productive way to work the fly.

My boss worked the river hard the first day. He never stopped casting the entire day. We had to drag him from the river to have lunch, and again at dinner. I know he was exhausted

Steelhead fishing the North Umpqua River, Oregon

135

Fighting a steelhead on Umpqua River

that night. I had divided my day between the rod and the camera, allowing my guide to fish. I had a great day even though I never touched a fish. My guide landed a nice little 6-pounder. Though it had started life in the river as a smolt from the hatchery, and was not one of the rare wild fish, he was still a bright, beautiful, hard-fighting fish. I got great images and was just as happy to photograph the show as to be the fisherman catching the fish.

Sunday was a repeat of the day before. My boss briefly had a fish on, but lost it in the swift current. I raced up and down the river trying to capture as much of it on film as I could. I fished some great water with no success, but I was thrilled. I had a new favorite river.

When we got into the office on Tuesday morning, my boss pulled me into his office first thing. He chewed me out up and down, wanting to know if I wanted to be a fishing product developer or a photographer. In his mind, we were there to test rods, learn new flies and new

North Umpqua River fly fishing, Oregon

137

techniques, and build better products. Though I had thousands of hours of fishing time logged on rivers, I couldn't argue. He was right. It put a damper on my elation.

Sometimes I am blinded by beauty, especially when it comes to rivers. It has always been a conflict for me, whether to fish or photograph. I know I have to do both. It is just who I am. It has always been that way and will never change. Oh, what a wonderful heartache it is.

The North Umpqua is a unique and special river. Its slick glides and deep narrow chutes make for some of the most treacherous wading of any river. Its steelhead are tough to catch and even harder to land in the small but brawling cascades and runs. Traditional fly casting can be difficult, and it often takes unorthodox methods to get the fly to the fish. The beauty of the river, the water, and the surrounding country is worth every hard-earned minute of time.

I have been back many times since that first "business trip" and have caught my fair share of fish, but I don't get there often enough. The place lives in my heart. I have a book that I keep with my favorites in a bookshelf in our

North Umpqua
River volcanic rock ledges

Releasing a bright silver steelhead

139

little den. It is called *North Umpqua* by noted photographer laureate of the Umpqua, Dan Callahan. I know Dan Callahan would have understood what I feel about this river. His book of photographs brims with the joy of the place.

Where flows the Umpqua? It flows in my heart. I know it flowed in his, too.

« *Mauves of sunset on ledges of upper Umpqua River*

North Umpqua River, misty evening light

*Where flows
the Umpqua*

CONSERVATION AND THE AMERICAN DREAM

Despite how advanced we seemed to have become as humans, how technically savvy we are, how many incredible innovations we take for granted in our everyday lives, we still need to be connected with something to feel whole and balanced. We can't lose sight of the fact we are still tied to the real rhythms of our natural world.

Beaverpond and Mount Moran, Grand Tetons, Wyoming

Saving wilderness for future generations to enjoy

From a geological perspective, as a species we are evolving faster than any other creature in our planet's history. We are like a shooting comet across the night sky. The problem with comets is that they come and go rather quickly.

It is imperative that we remember who we are and how we fit into this living planet. We are only one part of this wondrous natural garden called earth. As my wife constantly reminds me when I think I can do things outside the bounds of nature's laws, the fact is that we cannot break the laws of nature. In the end game, it is just not possible to trump nature. There are always consequences. As a species, we must realize the tremendous impact we are having on our own home planet.

Wild river, Baxter State Park, Maine

Trout fishing keeps me grounded. It helps me to stay connected to the earth, to my primordial past. Trout fishing in itself is the end product of a century of dedication by individuals and organizations—wise men and women who had the foresight to protect and keep large tracts of land wild and natural so that rivers can run pure and sustain natural populations of native species. Knowing there are wild trout and clear-flowing trout streams in the world gives me hope that maybe we can pass these treasures to generations to come.

No one individual can hope to manage all the environmental issues that confront us in the future. As individuals, we can simply try to tread as lightly as possible on the earth. As citizens, we can make our voices heard in the halls of Congress and in local meetings on the fate of our home streams. As the presiding members of the natural world, it is our duty to be the keepers of the wild land, fresh water, and clean air that are the birthrights of every member of the planet's population.

Wilderness lake,
Adirondack State Park,
New York

Wild Rocky Mountain
cutthroat trout

We have a grandson now, and I cannot wait to take him trout fishing. Quinn is all boy. He already knows about birds, deer, and rabbits and loves working in my garden with me. I know he will be fascinated with everything that goes into fly fishing. He will be two this spring and I hope to get him out with me on one of the smaller streams near our home.

I have spent my entire life fighting to keep rivers and streams wild and pure enough to maintain natural spawning populations of wild trout for my own children and for their children. Now that the first of their children are here, it brings home the reason why we have fought so hard to keep wilderness a part of our natural heritage. My grandson can enjoy the same experiences that my grandfather, my father, my children, and I have been able to experience.

147

Fly fishing on the Lamoille River, Vermont

I dreamed that one day our grandchildren would hike with us on wild mountain trails and wade pure, clear trout rivers with us. That day has come to pass.

The core of the American Dream has always been freedom. There is no better way to celebrate freedom than to preserve those real areas of wilderness we have left. This is our true American heritage and the legacy we will leave.

Fly fishing crystal-clear wild Alaskan river

DREAM OF THE WEST

It seems my whole life has been built around dreams of the West. As a kid, I played explorer and mountain man. I envisioned exploring every river and stream to its headwaters, wondering about all the amazing things I would find. I dreamed about the pure wildness when the lands of the West were only inhabited by Native Americans, bison and elk herds, and great flocks of wildfowl.

I imagined the feel of the earth and wind while standing in the tall grasses of the high plains, seeing for the first time in the western distance the front range of

Smith River overlook, Montana

the great Rocky Mountains. The visions of the wilderness West gave me a sense of connectedness to the earth and an appreciation for humanity's relationship to core natural elements.

In high school, the Vietnam War began to engulf our thoughts and changed our view of the world forever. Friends were coming back from the war with or without limbs, their fragile mental capacity diminished as they attempted to restart the lives they were just beginning to live. Knowing I could be one of them the following year, after graduation, put life in an entirely different perspective.

Fly fishing the Green River, Utah

Greedy cutthroat trout with sculpin and man-made fly

I had a hard time staying focused on academics. All I wanted to do was to be outdoors, to find wilderness and to find my place in the natural world, somewhere that men were not killing one another for whatever reason. This was for me, like thousands of other young people, a time that forced me to really look inside myself, to understand who I truly was as a human being, what I wanted most from my one life on this earth, how I wanted to live it, where and with whom to share my life. In that year after high school, waiting to be drafted or not, I was able to find a clear view of who I was and how I wanted to live my life.

Somehow my lottery number in the draft was high enough to keep me from going to the war. When I learned I was free, the West was foremost on my mind. The daydreams as a child were the fountainhead of my view of the future. I wanted to explore and experience every wild piece of country and the rivers and streams that dissected that wild country that still existed in the West.

Landing trout,
Roaring Fork River,
Colorado

For the next two summers, I roamed the West in an old pickup truck and homemade camper. I covered the Rocky Mountains from northern British Columbia to New Mexico. Places like Yellowstone, the Tetons, the Wind River Range, and Glacier and Rocky Mountain National Parks were finally touched and realized. Rivers with names from mountain men journals and *Outdoor Life* articles, such as the Green, Colorado, Madison, Firehole, and Roaring Fork, came into my life and forever touched my core.

I had a clear goal: to remain in the wilderness of the West as an environmentalist and outdoor photographer. I needed a college education. With mediocre high school grades, no scholarships were readily forthcoming. I would have to work my way through school—and then head straight back to the wilderness.

Fall reflections on Provo River, Utah

*Evening light, Boulder
River, Montana*

On my way back to the wilderness I took a slight turn at the fork in the road. Her name was Kate. My detour away from the West was only a temporary change in course. Over the next few years we supported each other through college, started our family, and headed back to the wilderness of the West.

Somehow over the years, together we have managed to stay true to our core goals. Wilderness, wild rivers, and living a life in harmony with the natural world are still guiding principles that light our pathway.

Reflected light on brook trout pool, Blue Ridge Mountains, Virginia

The clear, cold waters of the Gallatin River

Float fishing the Yellowstone River as it flows through Paradise Valley, Montana

We no longer live in the West, but those dreams still form our ideals, our reality. The way you choose to live your life can contain all your dreams, all your genius, and all your passions. We still dream of the West, but today the dream is more encompassing, grander, and without limits. It is called our future.

Square Top Mountain and headwaters of the Green River, Wind River Mountains, Wyoming

Acknowledgments

I want to thank Kate for her help, guidance, and initial editing in this adventure in trout waters. I also want to thank Nick Lyons who so graciously agreed to write the introduction to Trout Water. *It is a great privilege to share this space with Nick.*

Maroon Bells reflected in Maroon Lake, Aspen, Colorado

About The Author

Jim Rowinski *has spent his entire adult life in and around trout streams. He has devoted most of his career to designing and developing fly rods, reels, wading shoes, and other gear for the most prestigious brands in the industry. He has also been in the forefront of stream conservation for many years. In 1995, as the head of L.L. Bean Fly-fishing, Jim introduced the original Aqua Stealth sticky rubber-soled wading shoes to help stop the spread of whirling disease. Jim and L.L. Bean set up the first corporate sponsorship with The Whirling Disease Foundation to give a percentage of all Aqua Stealth sales to WDF to aid in the fight against whirling disease.*

Jim's passion for river photography has taken him around the globe. His photo credits include numerous national magazines, catalogs, calendars, and national ad campaigns. His credits also include books on outdoor photography and fly fishing. A former wilderness and river guide, Jim has taught photography and fly casting since 1982. You can see the entire spectrum of Jim's photographs on his Web site: www.JimRowinskiPhotography.com. He and his wife Kate live in beautiful Charlottesville, Virginia.